Praise

"Time Bandit addresses the key element of balance for individuals and teams. Understanding how to manage priorities and habits for the holistic view is powerful."

> – **Ken "Buck" Bryan,** Chief Information Officer, The Health Plan (THP)

"We coach salespeople new methods using social selling to deliver consistent results. The habit tracking and priority management in Time Bandit is a complimentary way to plan your time and outcomes."

> – **Brandon Lee,** CEO, FistBump

"Working on the most important and urgent priorities in sales, as with many professions, is the key to success. Layering in good habit-building makes the Time Bandit method a blueprint to deliver immediate and long-term sustained value."

— **Spencer O'Leary,**
CEO ActiveOps, North America

"Time Bandit an easy method to remind us how to stay focused on the important tasks, which is crucial for marketing teams, which typically deal with many disparate requests."

— **Jennifer Troxell,**
Chief Marketing Officer, pgEdge

Time Bandit

A simple method to prioritize your focus and energy to do more

Michael Cupps

R^ethink

First published in Great Britain in 2023
by Rethink Press (www.rethinkpress.com)

Contents

Foreword

Michael and I first met at Global 360 over fifteen years ago; ever since, I have appreciated his ability to understand the needs of internal and external clients, delivering results while maintaining a healthy work–life balance. As a professor, I tell my students that time is the most precious commodity that anyone has: once time is gone, you cannot buy it back. That is why I believe *Time Bandit* is so important, because it provides practical advice and tools to help you make the most of your time, both personally and professionally.

Early in my career I was selected to be part of the Bombardier Leadership Development Program. As emerging leaders, we were exposed to several leadership development opportunities; one such opportunity was on time management. In this session, we developed an understanding of our personal values and how to create value-based professional and personal goals. We also learned how to create and prioritize tasks on a daily basis that were aligned with our goals. I still use that method today, and Michael has modernized the approach for us with the Time Bandit method. His emphasis on priority management vs task management and the balance of work, personal and aspirational, is unique and pertinent. The accompanying app or a traditional notepad will allow you to apply the book's teachings in your daily life, enabling you to create good habits that will last you a lifetime.

Whether you're a student, business owner, or just someone looking to make the most of your time, I highly recommend this practical guide that can help you achieve your goals, build good habits and get rid of bad ones. *Time Bandit* is easy to comprehend and apply. Congratulations to Michael Cupps on writing such a valuable and insightful book.

Dr Zain Ali,
Professor at Neeley College of Business,
Texas Christian University

Introduction

Time is a precious commodity that we cannot recycle or retrieve, a resource that we all wish we had more of. And yet, while figuring out your direction and core responsibilities – crucial for personal and professional growth – how often do you feel as though your days and weeks are being hijacked? Time theft takes many forms, from interruptions by colleagues and family members to the ever-present digital disruptions that constantly pull your attention away from the task at hand. This is why we must learn to manage the time we have wisely. Whether you're leading a team, organizing a family, or managing your own life, it's essential to have a clear sense of direction and avoid distractions.

This is where *Time Bandit* comes in, offering a holistic system that can help you rationalize your time and prioritize your to-do list in a way that gets all aspects of your life and work in sync. The primary focus here is on individual productivity – I'm going to teach you how to take back control of your time and reduce those stubborn time wasters head-on.

I do not have a PhD in science, a massive social media following or academic expertise in human behavior. Yet growing up on a farm taught me the value of resourcefulness and creativity, as well as the importance of time management when dealing with the time-sensitive tasks involved in agriculture.

Since then, I have accumulated over thirty years of experience in the business world, including business-to-business (B2B) sales and marketing positions, both on the frontline as well as management and coaching roles. In this time, I have witnessed first-hand the rise of technology designed to make work more efficient. From commercial systems like SAP and Salesforce to productivity apps (MS Office) and various other software solutions, I've tried them all. In my experience, while they can certainly help, they often end up creating more silos, becoming overwhelming and difficult to navigate relative to your other tasks. Failure to connect these up in a usable way is a huge driver of inefficiency. But here's the thing: these systems aren't going away. In fact, they're critical to the flow of information and the centralization of data. So how do we balance the benefits of technology with the need for simplicity and ease of use?

In the following pages, I will illuminate why some productivity systems have been success-ful in certain tasks, roles and outcomes, but others haven't. Then, I will introduce a system that can help anyone to manage their tasks and time. While the system may not extinguish all time wasted, it will help you control and man-age them, while the concepts presented will broaden your understanding of the diverse aspects of the 'to-do list'. Overall, it provides a dependable method to classify, prioritize and handle all the tasks that confront you on a daily, weekly and monthly basis – both in your pro-fessional and personal life, including your aspi-rations. Beyond the individual, teams big and small can make efficient use of it.

Through a comprehensive method, I'll show you how to categorize and rank your tasks and habits, giving you the power to decide when and why you work on certain things. By developing a better understanding of your priorities and goals, you'll be able to minimize the impact of distractions and stay focused on what genuinely matters.

Let's be real: whether it's keeping track of our personal schedules or managing our work-loads, we all need a system that works for us. Personally, I've tended to rely more on good old-fashioned pen and paper. Sure, there are plenty of apps and tools out there, but I've always gone back to the trusty paper to-do list, which, for me, is reliable and effective. It's how I started, before eventually transitioning to a spreadsheet and then automating more of my workflow. It's why we offer both an app and a physical notepad for the Time Bandit method – in this book, I draw on my own experiences and suggestions to help you find a system that works for you.

Time Bandit will help you tackle a unique challenge: time wasters. It's a practical and comprehensive guide that will teach you how to manage your time more effectively, guard against the distractions and interruptions that rob you of precious hours to help you achieve greater peace of mind and fulfillment. Whether you're a busy professional or an aspiring learner, a parent juggling multiple responsibilities or simply someone who wants to take control of their time, *Time Bandit* will help you reclaim your time and stay on top of your goals.

If you're seeking to achieve greater productivity and balance, join me on this journey and learn how to stop wasting time on the wrong things once and for all. I understand that your time is valuable and I don't want to waste it with unnecessary theory. For this reason, the book is deliberately concise. If you're ready to take control of your schedule and maximize your productivity, let's get started.

ONE

The Concept Of Time Theft

Once time has been spent, we cannot replenish it, which is why it is important to manage time effectively to achieve personal and professional goals. However, there are many distractions and obstacles that can hinder effective time management. These are what I call 'wasters'.

Time

Time is a non-renewable resource. Once it's gone, it's gone. This realization can be mentally challenging for people. At a macro level, we need to determine how much time we spend on work, our personal life (including sleeping) and our aspirations – the things we want to do or become. At a micro level, we struggle to balance our big-picture plans with the constant demands of everyday life. Each day, we have a finite number of hours and minutes to accomplish all of our tasks and maintain our habits. We'll discuss the difference between habits and tasks later.

Meanwhile, there are deadlines to juggle. A deadline is a time limit within which a particular task must be completed. The business demands a delivery date; the doctor sets an appointment time; you plan around an important milestone such as a birthday or a vacation that cannot be moved. Events aside, setting deadlines for all the tasks on your to-do list is not always a straightforward process – though businesses may have to adhere to timed service level agreements or regulatory demands, many tasks assigned to you should fit into your schedule of importance and urgency while still aligning your efforts to the team and project.

Another important element of time to consider is your schedule. While you may not have complete control over your schedule, you can learn how to say 'no' more often and take ownership of your time. Businesses usually have a schedule for everyone to follow, with customer activities, meetings and sales forecasts that need to be done at particular points. Outside of work, there are other schedules to factor in, too, such as school events, health check-ups and holidays. It can be a juggling act at times, which is exactly what defines the need to get your priorities identified correctly, allowing you to rise above the chaos.

Your goal is to become efficient at identifying how much time you should allocate to each task and habit based on your priorities. This ability often comes with experience, but you can learn and adjust along the way. The key factor is understanding what your time constraints and priorities are. When you can do this, you can better meet your deadlines – we will explore this in greater detail in a later chapter.

Time wasters

Time wasters can take many forms, but they all share the common trait of stealing time away from important tasks or activities. For example, social media can waste a lot of time if used excessively and will rob us of productive work time. Other wasters include interruptions from co-workers, email overload and procrastination.

To effectively manage time wasters, it is important to understand their underlying causes. Often, losing time results from poor planning, lack of focus or misunderstood priorities. For example, if an individual does not clearly understand the importance of prioritizing, they may waste time on low-value tasks or become overwhelmed by too many tasks.

Identifying the wasters

You must be aware of time wasters so that you can take steps to avoid them and make more effective use of your time. Below are some examples of common wasters that can prevent you from being productive:

- **Interruptions** are one of the most common wasters in the workplace. Interruptions prevent you from staying on track with your work.

- **Procrastination** is the tendency to put off important tasks and instead focus on less important or urgent ones.

- **Multitasking** is the practice of doing multiple tasks at once, which can actually be counterproductive. When you multi-task, your brain is constantly switching between tasks, which can make it difficult to concentrate and may lead to mistakes.

- **Meetings** waste a lot of time when they are unnecessary or not planned well.

- **Social media** has the potential to be a huge waste of time, particularly if you scroll through your feeds for hours on end.

- **Email overload** takes up a significant amount of time each day.

- **Digital disruptions** may be considered cool by management experts, but they can be an enormous waste of time and decrease productivity. According to the Information Overload Research Group, knowledge workers in the US waste a staggering 25% of their time dealing with data streams, costing the economy almost a trillion dollars annually.[1]

Roles

The goal of this book is to help you find a way to use schedules, deadlines and priorities to

---

1   L Rosen and A Samuel, 'Conquering digital distraction', *Harvard Business Review* (June 2015), https://hbr.org/2015 /06/conquering-digital-distraction, accessed June 2023

allocate your time efficiently and comfortably. By taking control of your schedule and understanding the deadlines and priorities of your tasks, you can create a more balanced and productive life. Part of that process is identifying our roles, an important aspect of our lives. For easier management, it's helpful to categorize these into three main areas: your personal role, business role and aspirational role.

Personal role

The personal role pertains to your home life, health and hobbies. It's crucial to prioritize and schedule time for these parts of your life, whether that's activities like reading, dog walking or attending yoga classes, as they are important for maintaining healthy relationships, staying physically fit and enjoying life.

Many people overlook the importance of their personal needs when planning their days, weeks and months. But it's essential not to neglect this aspect of your life, as your loved ones depend on you, and taking a break from work to pursue personal interests is beneficial for your mental health. If you're able to keep two separate to-do lists for personal and business tasks, that's great. However, in my experience, most people need a central repository to manage and balance everything effectively.

Managing your personal role is just as important as managing your business and aspirational roles. By prioritizing and scheduling time for all three roles, you'll be able to achieve a more balanced and fulfilling life.

Business role

As mentioned earlier, your role in business can take many forms. Whether you work for a company, are self-employed or a business owner, you likely have a lengthy to-do list. That can be overwhelming. It can be discouraging to see the same tasks on your list week after week. Your business-related tasks will fall into different categories, such as one-off tasks, tasks within a project, or business-as-usual (BAU) tasks. BAU tasks are the ones you have to do to keep your business running smoothly. You may want to turn some of your BAU tasks into habits to streamline your workflow. In the upcoming section, we will delve further into this.

Aspirational role

The aspirational role often gets neglected in our daily and weekly routines. We keep planning to get to it but then we don't, or we suffer from 'maybe someday' syndrome. Yet this role is vital for your long-term motivation and peace of mind. I am not a doctor, but I can do research, and there are plenty of stories, books and programs on the benefits of fulfilling aspirations and the inspiration it provides.

Aspiration schedules are often overlooked, but are just as important as work and personal schedules. Pursuing your dreams and goals can sometimes feel selfish, but it's essential to prioritize and allocate time to them. Rather than put your aspirational role on the back burner, find a passion that you can schedule time for. Be your own Time Bandit and protect your time. Whether it's playing music for thirty minutes a week or learning a new language, make sure you fit it into your plans.

Take control

Time wasters all rob us of our time, but they come in many forms, with varying degrees of intent. They may be well-intentioned or ill-intentioned, but regardless of their motivation, they all have the same effect of eating away at our productivity and stealing valuable time. If not managed, they have us focusing on tasks that are not urgent or important, while ignoring more pressing matters.

To combat a waste of time slipping into your day, I propose a system that enables you to become your own Time Bandit. A system that helps you to take back your time by identifying and eliminating the sources of distraction that are interfering with your productivity. Your Time Bandit aids you in managing the tasks ahead, keeping you focused and productive and avoiding the trap of distraction.

Assuming that we need eight hours of sleep each night, we are left with sixteen hours a day to balance the various aspects of our lives, including our personal, work and aspirational roles. But it is all too easy to get thrown off balance by the constant barrage of interruptions that we face on a daily basis. Applying this system to your to-do list helps you maintain this balance by providing you with the tools and strategies you need to overcome these distractions and stay on track.

Summary

By practicing better priority management and using the Time Bandit method to avoid being distracted by things that aren't a priority, you can achieve a better work–life balance and reduce anxiety. With more time for your personal and professional obligations, you can enjoy a more fulfilling and productive life.

TWO

Habits, Tasks And Projects

A habit is a repeated behavior or action that has become automatic because of frequent repetition. We form habits through repeated experiences, and they can be positive or negative.

Building habits

Often, to-do lists can become cluttered with things you already do, things you want to do, and habits you want to stop or start. These things are, or should become, habits rather than tasks (to dos). On a personal level, they could include activities like walking the dog at 6am, setting up your weekly to-do list every Sunday, or following a daily fitness routine. Examples of habits designed to stop certain things could be to quit smoking or limit social media time. On the business side, it could involve specific job-related tasks you need to do every day. For instance, if you work in sales, you may need to reach out to five new contacts each day or monitor web traffic to check if your clients are visiting your website. In sales, establishing good habits and breaking bad ones can make a big difference to your performance. In your aspirational role, building habits is how you make time to pursue your passion and engage in activities that inspire you. This could mean setting aside time each day to write, practice a new language, or meditate in a peaceful environment.

Have you ever felt envious of those who seem to achieve their goals with ease? The secret is not in having some extraordinary talent, but in having a well-defined system and using the right tools. A habit tracker, combined with the power of streak accountability, is one such tool that can help you easily reach your goals. A habit tracker is a personal objective-setting and tracking tool; as the name suggests, it helps you keep track of any habits you wish to build into your life, from working out a certain number of times per week to limiting your time spent on social media. You input the details of your goals into the system and, as you make progress, you can see how close you are to achieving them. This way, you can adjust your approach to ensure you're consistently moving toward your objectives.

Streak accountability is key to using a habit tracker effectively. It involves achieving a streak of unbroken successes with a specific behavior or goal over a certain period. According to the UK company Growth Engineering: 'Completing (or continuing) a streak usually triggers a dopamine boost. But streaks are powerful because breaking them feels soul-achingly awful. Avoiding this sensation can create its own form of incentive.'[2]

Having a streak provides motivation to continue the positive habit and gives you something to maintain. Even if you break your streak, trying to set a better one can motivate you to start again and persist until you reach your goals. Using a habit tracker alongside streak accountability will help you to establish and

---

2   'What are Streaks and why do they work?', (Growth Engineering Blog, 13 March 2019), www.growthengineering.co.uk/what-are-streaks, accessed June 2023.

maintain new habits that contribute to the achievement of your long-term goals.

Habit tracking is a simple step that can make a big difference in reaching your goals, but it's more than just a tick-box exercise – it's about analyzing trends in the data to see patterns and make better decisions for future improvements. For example, you can judge when it's time to increase your goals and challenge yourself further. Don't forget to celebrate your successes – setting reminders and celebrating your accomplishments encourages you to stay enthusiastic and keep your long-term objectives in mind. Practicing gratitude by recognizing your progress also boosts your confidence and overall well-being. Whether you're working toward short-term or long-term goals, a habit tracker can help you get there with ease.

Habit stacking

The concept of habit stacking, also known as habit chaining, is a strategy that aims to leverage existing habits as a way to build new ones. By linking the new habit to an existing one, you create a mental association that helps reinforce the new behavior.

The key to building and maintaining strong habits is consistency. Whether you're trying to establish new habits or break bad ones, keeping track of your progress can make all the difference in achieving your goals.

Personally, I find James Clear's approach, which he sets out in *Atomic Habits*, to be incredibly helpful for building, breaking and stacking habits in a healthy and accountable way.[3] There are many other sources of expertise on this topic, but in this book we will focus on the simple approach of habit tracking. You are, of course, free to manage your habits in whatever way works best for your schedule and behavior patterns – the latter being the most important factor.

It will be useful to familiarize yourself with the practice of habit stacking, which habit trackers can help with. If you don't already have a habit tracker from another source, you can quickly set one up using popular tools. Consistency is key, and tracking your progress is essential for making long-term habit adoption possible.

---

3   J Clear, *Atomic Habits* (Avery, 2018)

Seeing a visual representation of your efforts (and sometimes missteps) can be incredibly motivating.

Tasks

Task management is a complex undertaking that has inspired millions of dollars' worth of research, technology and consulting services. The rise of robotic process automation (RPA) is a testament to the fact that, these days, we need to complete more tasks, faster and with greater accuracy. Research firm Forrester expects the RPA market to reach $22 billion by 2025.[4]

In the context of personal improvement, I define a 'task' as something that you need to

---

4   VB Templeman, 'RPA market to reach $22 billion by 2025: Forrester', (Digital Nation, 2 March 2022), www.digitalnationaus.com.au/news/rpa-market-to-reach-22-billion-by-2025-forrester-576764, accessed June 2023

do. Whether it's simple or complex, has a deadline or not, it requires your attention, time and effort to complete. It may be that some tasks eventually become ingrained as habits. Regardless, you likely have many tasks to manage and prioritizing them correctly is a critical aspect of your daily and weekly routines. If you're approaching task management from a team perspective, tasks are likely the primary commodity that you're managing, whether you like it or not.

In the Time Bandit methodology, a task is a piece of work or activity that needs to be accomplished. It is a specific, defined piece of effort with an obvious goal and outcome, typically (but not necessarily) with a deadline. A task is something with a clear beginning and end. Tasks can come in many forms, such as scheduling a dentist appointment or sending an introductory sales letter. The challenge is to break these tasks down into distinct parts and schedule them accordingly.

We also have things we must do daily, weekly, or routinely just to keep things running. We'll refer to these as BAU tasks. It's important to schedule these work tasks and integrate them into your day, as they are non-negotiable. Ideally, load and schedule BAU tasks in a system of record, rather than an external task management system. For sales, this might be a CRM tool, while for other industries it could be an ERP or claims system. For the personal role, it may be using your car to drive the kids to school – a different role, but it is equally important to plan ahead. Assuming you have a method for your BAU, the only tracking needed is the time allotted to it in your schedule.

Consider the example of cold calling in sales. If your job is telemarketing, you probably come

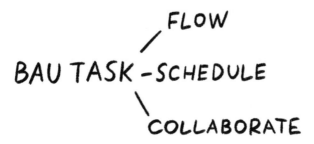

into work with a list of names and numbers to call or email. These would be BAU tasks and, if your company or manager is doing things right, they should have a reasonable expectation regarding the volume and frequency of these tasks. For, say, two hours of your workday, you dial from a pre-determined list.

Another example is claims processing. Adjusters may have a reasonable expectation of completing twelve claims per day; based on this, you can schedule 5.4 hours of your workday to completing these core activities. You could then dedicate the remaining time in your schedule to handling exception tasks, training or attending meetings. While you don't need to account for these tasks individually, you still need to block off uninterruptible time in your schedule. Your tasks outside of BAU are the ones that you need to track and prioritize, as much of your time is already being consumed by BAU tasks.

In an Adobe survey, respondents reported spending an average of 209 minutes of their workday checking their work email and 143 minutes checking their personal email, for a total of 352 minutes (about five hours and fifty-two minutes) each day.[5]

One method to increase your efficiency at completing tasks and BAU is 'task binding', which is

---

5   A Johnson Hess, 'Here's how many hours American workers spend on email each day', (CNBC, 22 September 2019), www.cnbc.com/2019/09/22/heres-how-many-hours-american-workers-spend-on-email-each-day.html, accessed June 2023.

much like habit stacking. To task bind, identify similar activities and plan to get them all done in a reasonable time period. For example, I use Microsoft's Viva messaging block, a great formula to catch up on email. Then find more 'like' tasks and bind them into a single time block. Account research is a good example in sales. For an active social media influencer, you might block time to write future posts. Instead of aimlessly scrolling others, sit down and write your next ten to twenty posts.

Projects

Projects, like tasks, are limited in time but they have a particular, larger purpose, often with a desired outcome, budget and timeline. They are bigger than tasks, though, and usually comprise a series of tasks that must be completed to solve a problem, create a product or meet a specific need. The line can be blurred between what is a task versus a project, being a wider set of activities completed with a view to accomplishing a logical goal.

While it's thrilling to take part in or even lead a project, it is a sobering reality that most business projects fall short of expectations. *Harvard Business Review* research shows that only 35% of the projects undertaken worldwide are successful.[6] This means we're wasting an extravagant amount of time, money and opportunity, which often results in dwindling interest and a failure to even complete a project. Yet when they succeed, we value projects highly and use them as benchmarks for future endeavors.

---

6   Nieto-Rodriguez, A, 'The Project Economy Has Arrived', A Nieto-Rodriguez, 'The project economy has arrived', *Harvard Business Review* (November–December 2021), https://hbr.org/2021/11/the-project-economy-has -arrived, accessed June 2023.

Projects can be exciting and rewarding, but are also time-consuming and stressful. If you are feeling stressed out because of the many tasks involved in and results needed for a project, break down your projects into a series of manageable tasks, with clear outcomes and deadlines, and prioritize them based on their urgency and importance, just as you would with any other task. This approach ensures that everyone involved understands their role and knows what is expected of them.

If a project lacks defined tasks or is missing key resources, trouble can arise. Doubt creeps in and, before long, everyone questions why they're even involved. To avoid this, make sure each project has a clear list of tasks and the relevant parties have the resources to complete them.

Remember, projects do not differ from other tasks. You should manage and prioritize them with the same rigor and attention to detail as every task on your list. By breaking down your projects into manageable tasks and prioritizing them, you can ensure completion on time and to the best of your ability. Next time you are faced with a daunting project, take a deep breath and break it down into smaller, more manageable pieces.

Summary

To avoid losing time, it's important to differentiate between tasks and other routine activities, such as BAU and habits. Tasks should have an obvious goal and deadline and will require dedicated time for execution. This will help you prioritize and focus on the most important activities and avoid the time wasters.

Tracking and improving our habits requires more than just inputting information into an app or spreadsheet. It requires commitment to consistent strategies that help us achieve our goals quickly and easily. Combining a habit tracker with streak accountability is a powerful tool that can help you stay motivated and on track. Celebrating small wins and consistently making progress can improve well-being, motivation and creativity.

It's crucial to recognize the significant differences between the various kinds of tasks on your to-do list. Failure to do so is often the reason to-do lists don't work. If you don't give the tasks a label (eg personal, BAU, project) and make a plan, they'll just end up on a messy list of stuff that needs doing. By categorizing the tasks, you can mentally prepare yourself to tackle them when the time is right. Get into that habit.

THREE

Solving The Puzzle Of A Multidimensional Life

Think of your life as a Rubik's Cube. Time Bandit focuses on the layer between the person and all the tasks they need to accomplish, regardless of what role they relate to. Its purpose is to allow you to systematically prioritize the way in which you engage with various tasks and habits so that all sides of your cube align.

Time management

Managing time can be a real challenge, especially when there are countless tasks and habits to keep track of. With only twenty-four hours in a day and seven days in a week, it's easy to feel overwhelmed. Don't worry, you don't need to schedule every minute of every day to be productive. It's important to remember that we cannot plan some of the most fulfilling moments in life. Whether it's a conversation with a friend or a peaceful moment under the full moon, some of the most precious things are spontaneous and unscheduled. It's important to balance work and play, which is why this book and method aim to help you become your own bandit, managing your time in a way that's both efficient and flexible. So go ahead, live a little.

Finding a solution to the time-management puzzle requires a strategic approach. By organizing our habits and tasks into categories based on priority and effort required, we can balance productivity and enjoyment of life. But it's important to remember that perfection is not the goal. Instead, we should set realistic expectations and be honest about what truly deserves our urgent attention versus what is important but can wait. Don't let others dictate your schedule; protect your time by setting boundaries and prioritizing your own needs.

The Time Bandit method isn't a scientifically proven formula, but it will help you understand how to prioritize, a method that allows you to easily categorize events as either habits or tasks, with clear metrics for urgency and importance based on the role they play in your life. This system empowers you to adapt your days, weeks and months to accommodate the goals you set for yourself. The best part is it's completely flexible: as your priorities change and your goals grow, you can adjust your schedule accordingly. Whether you're training for a marathon or gearing up for the holiday season, you can be the master of your own time. While there are plenty of helpful tech tools out there, nothing can replace your personal judgment and decision-making when it comes to prioritization and time management.

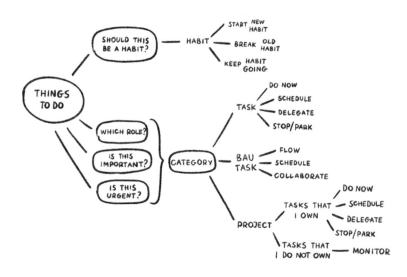

The middleware

You may well have felt a tinge of anxiety about how to achieve balance in your life – a goal that eludes many. Some people become so engrossed in one aspect of their life that they neglect others, while some give up on their dreams altogether. Still others soldier on, trying to improve despite the hurdles.

In my earlier years, I had the pleasure of working for webMethods, a middleware company. Our solutions focused on connecting various systems and data within a company to create a smoother, more integrated experience. This could be anything from streamlining supply chain operations to optimizing finance and HR departments. Keep in mind that we weren't the actual systems or data involved; we were the bridge that linked them together. To make this work, we relied on two critical components: a map and a protocol. We helped the system on the other end interpret the information (the protocol) in its own language and follow the steps (the map) to ensure a secure and accurate transaction when an electronic order was placed.

Managing our to-do list can be overwhelming, but what if we could become our own middleware for the universe of tasks? The goal isn't to replace the systems you currently use to complete transactions – things like calendars, project management boards, CRMs, ERPs and all the other tools you rely on will still be the system of record. Instead, the goal is to help you prioritize your allocation of time and effort to each task, accurately and in a timely way.

The priority manager

Note the term priority manager, not task manager. This is because it's the protocol and the map that matter, not the actual task itself. The aim is to improve the flow of your daily tasks, from mailing a birthday card, attending meetings, going for a run, to uploading spreadsheets. You'll still have to complete the tasks, but you'll have a better system of control.

Your Time Bandit comprises a series of decisions that you schedule and prioritize in a whole new way. It's a system that allows you to allocate your time to meet the priority and deadlines required of each task. If you're effective at entering the tasks with the right variables and map them to your available resources, you'll be able to identify where to spend your time and, equally important, where not to. You can say goodbye to feeling overwhelmed and hello to a more productive, streamlined way of managing your tasks. With the priority manager, you can take control of your to-do list and achieve balance in all areas of your life.

Technology has become an essential asset in our daily lives, revolutionizing the way we live, work and communicate. But it's sometimes easy to get caught up in the distraction of it, for example by spending too much time scrolling through social media platforms like TikTok and Twitter.

The most important thing you need to understand and train yourself in is your realistic expectations. It's up to you to decide what you can get done in a day, week or month. Your body is a powerful tool that speaks to you – when you need sleep, nourishment or exercise, your body will let you know. You'll know when you need to focus your brainpower on work and when it's time to indulge in some nonsense.

Another rule of Time Bandit is to pay attention to your body's signals. It's important not to over commit or under commit yourself. You need to measure your capacity for pleasure, pain, gain and other factors. It's all about finding a balance that works for you, and that starts with understanding your limitations and expectations.

Take control of your time and make the most of it by listening to your body and setting realistic expectations for yourself. Don't let technology or other distractions steal your time and energy. With a little self-awareness and discipline, you can achieve balance and take charge.

Eisenhower Matrix

Crucial to the Time Bandit method is learning how to properly sort tasks, or anything that demands your time. One of the most effective strategies for managing time is to establish clear priorities and goals. For this purpose, you should focus on the important and urgent tasks first, and then follow a priority model that helps you forge a path to productivity. The way you initially approach categorizing or examining your tasks can either make or break your efforts toward productivity and efficiency. Understanding this fundamental principle can help you stay on track and achieve your goals; by categorizing your tasks correctly, you can ensure that you are focusing on the right things and making the most of your time.

As bestselling author, Nora Roberts, once reportedly said: 'The key to juggling is to know that some of the balls you have in the air are made of plastic and some are made of glass. You have to know which balls are glass and which are plastic and prioritize catching the glass ones.'[7]

---

7   JL Barnes (@jenlynnbarnes), 'One time, I was at a Q&A with Nora Roberts…' (23 January 2020), https://twitter .com/jenlynnbarnes/status/1220182162118451200?lang=en, accessed June 2023

Priorities are essential for everyone, but getting them right can be overwhelming for busy individuals or teams. Luckily, there's a solution: the Eisenhower Matrix.[8] This straightforward yet effective tool helps you prioritize your tasks, make informed decisions and take charge of your day. It helps you easily determine which tasks need your immediate attention (Do Now), which should be scheduled for later (Schedule), which can be given to someone else (Delegate), and which should be eliminated (Stop!). With the Eisenhower Matrix, you can focus on what actually matters now, increase your productivity and regain control over your time.

What exactly is the Eisenhower Matrix? Named after Dwight D Eisenhower, it is a powerful tool comprising four quadrants that represent different priority characteristics:

---

8   SR Covey, *The 7 Habits of Highly Effective People* (Simon & Schuster, 1999)

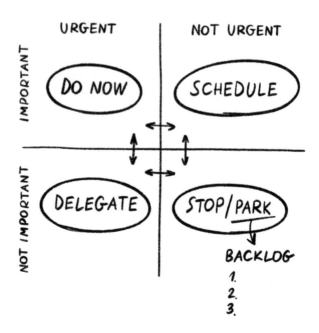

- Urgent/Important

- Not Urgent/Important

- Urgent/Not Important

- Not Urgent/Not Important

The Urgent/Important quadrant includes tasks that are important and require immediate attention, such as meeting urgent deadlines, crisis management and client calls. You should prioritize and complete these tasks first.

The Not Urgent/Important quadrant contains tasks that are important but not urgent, such as planning future projects or preparing for a scheduled meeting three weeks away. We must not ignore these tasks as they are critical for long-term success, despite their lack of urgency.

Answering emails or attending unnecessary meetings are examples of tasks that fall into the Urgent/Not Important quadrant and would require immediate attention but are not necessarily beneficial. Avoid these tasks if possible, as they consume time that could otherwise be used for more important tasks. Sometimes you can't avoid them, so do your best to handle them expeditiously. The best way to deal with these tasks may be to delegate them elsewhere.

Finally, stay away from the Not Urgent/Not Important quadrant – things like endlessly scrolling through social media or working on tasks that have no obvious goal and just kill time. While it's important to take breaks from being productive, eliminating these activities can help you make the most of your time.

Delegation and outsourcing are key components of effective time management. As Dwight D Eisenhower famously said, 'What is important is seldom urgent, and what is urgent is seldom important.'[9] By delegating or outsourcing

9   DD Eisenhower, 'Address at the Second Assembly of the World Council of Churches', Illinois, 19 August 1954 (The American Presidency Project), www.presidency.ucsb.edu/documents/address-the-second-assembly-the-world-council-churches-evanston-illinois, accessed June 2023.

less important tasks, you can focus on what matters most to you and maximize your productivity with minimal effort.

Summary

Ultimately, mastering time management isn't just about increasing productivity – it also leads to a more fulfilling life by helping you prioritize the important tasks in the most efficient way. Don't let time manage you; take control of your day and make the most of every moment.

FOUR

Becoming Your Own Time Bandit

No matter your role, it's crucial to treat all requests with the same level of attention, recognizing that we are limited by time and competing priorities. If an additional request is more important or urgent than what you're currently working on, other things may need to shift accordingly.

Taking charge

Now that you understand the importance of categorizing and prioritizing items by type, let's talk about how to handle new requests that come your way.

When something new arises, prioritize it as soon as possible by assessing its importance and urgency and placing it in the relevant quadrant of the Eisenhower Matrix. If the task falls into the 'schedule' section, assign it a deadline or put it in your calendar. If the task will be delegated, either do so immediately or plan to address it during your next review of your to-do list. If it is something not worth doing, delete it, but notify the requester. If it is interesting but not important or urgent now, park it on your backlog.

If you don't prioritize new tasks quickly, they can easily get lost or added to your already long task list. Take action immediately or risk the consequences later. If someone tries to give you more work when you're already working on a priority task, politely decline or delay the request and schedule a time to discuss it later. Of course, there will be exceptions to this rule, such as emergency situations involving your family or personal life.

The rhythm of priorities

Mastering the art of organizing and prioritizing tasks is crucial to combat the time-wasting activities. But time has a way of throwing unexpected challenges our way, and priorities can shift at any moment. That's why it's essential to establish a sustainable rhythm that allows your task list to develop with the appropriate importance and urgency. Most time-management gurus suggest re-evaluating your task list either weekly or daily. Daily is good practice, but it depends on your level of interest and attention to detail. If your life entails a lot of frequent changes, daily review is best. But if you're in a longer-term role like project management or enterprise sales, weekly reviews may suffice. If you opt for daily reviews, you should allocate just ten to fifteen minutes per day, while weekly reviews might require twenty to thirty minutes.

To establish this as a consistent habit, it's rec-ommended to either review your tasks and priorities before the day/week begins or at the end of each day/week. Most importantly, you need to choose a path and stay on it by making that time for it every day/week and scheduling it on your calendar in advance. With a rhythm established, you'll be able to stay ahead of your tasks and manage your time like a pro.

During your review of tasks and priorities, make adjustments as needed. For instance, look at your tasks to see if any deadlines are coming up that would make them more urgent. Alternatively, macro decisions by others may reduce the importance of a task, leading you to remove it, delay it or shift it to a delegate or park category. The goal is to ensure that your task list remains up-to-date and aligned with your goals. If this type of prioritization and organization of your time is completely new to you, I would recommend a daily review of your tasks just after you complete your daily habit tracker. Whether you choose morning (my preferred option, to start the day with a productive mindset) or the evening, review your schedule for the upcoming day to assess what time you have on your hands. Keep it simple: review the due date, importance and urgency of each task, and adjust as needed. Once you get into the rhythm of doing this, this will become as much of a habit as your morning coffee.

Your schedule

'We have so many meetings and calls that it's tough to stay focused. Meetings where you discuss mundane topics and abstractions are the enemies of productivity.'[10]

---

10   J Fried and D Heinemeier Hansson, *ReWork* (Random House, 2010)

Protecting your schedule can be a daunting task, especially in the post-pandemic work environment. As back-to-back video calls became the new normal in the Covid-19 lockdowns, it became routine to check in on colleagues and have some social interaction, even if it wasn't necessary. While some people found this enjoyable, others found it overwhelming. Regardless, we all had to adapt to an unprecedented situation.

Now that lockdowns have lifted and we've returned to a semblance of normalcy, it's crucial to regain control of your schedule. Time blocking is an effective way to do this. Time blocking involves setting aside specific time slots for your essential tasks, protecting them from distractions and interruptions.

Microsoft's Viva product is an excellent tool with which to apply this method. It enables you to predict and allocate time for focus or for responding to messages, making it easier to ensure you get time for both unique tasks and your everyday work. You should also include time for personal activities – in my experience, the pandemic conditioned people to disregard boundaries and steal your time without considering your workload or personal life.

As part of your scheduling, I recommend you reduce the length of your meetings to either twenty-five or fifty minutes, instead of half or full hours, giving you time for a quick break or refreshment. Remember, your schedule is your own to control.

If you travel for business, block out your travel time to avoid any mishaps or distractions arising that could detract from your focus. There's nothing worse than mentally dealing with an issue from an existing customer while walking into a meeting with a potential new one.

In scheduling, it's crucial to book in the non-negotiable tasks first, regardless of what role they relate to (personal, work, or aspirational). For instance, if you need to pick up your kids from school, block that time off in your schedule. We've discussed how BAU tasks require scheduling blocks, but it's essential to include your aspirations in your time blocking as well.

Unfortunately, aspirations are often the first to go when time is tight, but I urge you to block some time every week for tasks that contribute to your aspirations. It may seem small, but it will have a compounding effect. First, it will provide you with an opportunity to unwind and detach from personal and work-related challenges. Second, even if you spend just an hour a week working on your aspiration, this will add up and bring you closer to achieving your goal. In contrast, skipping it will leave you feeling uninspired and stuck in a rut.

Multi-task and multi-people projects

Multi-task and multi-people projects are a common occurrence in many industries and fields, and they can be both challenging and rewarding. In these types of projects, multiple tasks must be completed simultaneously, often involving people with different skill sets and areas of expertise. Successful completion of these projects requires effective communication, collaboration and project management skills.

One of the key challenges of projects is coordinating and prioritizing tasks. In projects comprising various tasks that need to be completed over the same timeline, it's difficult to determine which tasks are most important and which ones can wait. This is especially difficult when multiple people are involved, as each person may have a different perspective on what is most important. Managing team dynamics is a particular challenge in projects. When working with a team of people, there are likely to be differences in personalities, work styles and communication preferences, which can lead to conflict or misunderstandings. It is important to establish clear expectations for communication and collaboration and to address any conflicts or issues that arise in a timely and professional manner. In many cases, agreeing on task importance and urgency is the common language (protocol) that is needed. Effective communication is essential for the success of projects. This includes not only clear and concise communication among team members but also communication with stakeholders, clients and other external parties.

It is also important to establish the same priority manager from the outset. This can involve creating a plan that shows when tasks are due, what needs to be done and who is responsible for each task, as well as marking which tasks are most important and need to be done first. Regular meetings and communication among team members can also help ensure necessary adjustments that everyone agrees on are made and that tasks are being completed in a prioritized and efficient manner.

To avoid complex projects becoming overwhelming, you should break them down and own the parts that relate to you and your schedule. Many companies use third-party tools and software products that create yet another list for you, but these can be useful for managing projects. These tools can help with task management, scheduling, resource allocation and communication. Some also have templates for the Eisenhower Matrix. Examples of project management tools include Asana, Trello and Jira.

The key to success is using project management solutions that allow for easy tracking of assigned tasks and deadlines, integrating your own tasks with those from the other system and making sure they align with your priorities. Whether it's Monday.com, Asana, Microsoft Planner, or a unique solution tailored to your line of work, these systems can help ensure that each critical part of the project is owned and completed by the right person. For tasks with multiple steps that fall solely on your shoulders, you'll have to decide the sequence and time needed and determine if tasks can be done in any order or need a step-by-step process. Use Time Bandit as your middleware to identify your tasks that contribute to a project. There is no need to let complex projects overwhelm you – with the right tools and strategies, you can tackle anything that comes your way.

I want to emphasize again that one of the main reasons we struggle with organization and efficiency is because we have too many places to find or complete our work. To avoid this, it's important to categorize tasks and ensure they are easily accessible if they don't fall within our usual daily activities. For your own time and priorities, continue to utilize Time Bandit to manage your tasks. Also ensure that all other tasks are included in this prioritization matrix and targeted with the right level of urgency and importance using the same prioritization you would for other tasks – be sure to Do Now, Schedule and Delegate. Keeping your own time and tasks prioritized will keep the project in motion – at least the parts that you own.

By working together, team members can leverage their strengths and expertise to achieve better results than they could on their own. Be sure to recognize and reward team members for their contributions to a project. Even just saying, 'Good job' to a peer, matters.

Summary

It is up to you to control your schedule. Using the time blocking method and prioritizing non-negotiable tasks, including aspirations, is essential for effective scheduling. Blocking off time, no matter how little, for your aspirations every week will help you achieve your goals and maintain a healthy work–life balance.

Remember, it's up to you to protect your time and your task list. Discipline yourself, stay diligent and don't hesitate to say 'No' when necessary. People will trust you when you deliver for them on time and with care.

Complex projects can be both challenging and rewarding. They require effective communication, collaboration and prioritization to be successful. By establishing clear goals and priorities, managing team dynamics and leveraging project management tools, team members can work together toward better outcomes and grow both individually and as a team.

FIVE

Tracking Your Progress

How can we optimize the use of apps to improve our productivity? With so many apps available, it's difficult to determine which ones are truly helpful. The good news is that they can be incredibly useful if we approach them with a middleware mindset to prioritize and categorize our time and tasks.

Apps, apps everywhere

With so many productivity tools available, the choice of which to use can be overwhelming. From Slack to Teams, Asana to Salesforce, each claims to streamline your time and tasks. But these tools can only help to a certain extent. As much as we prioritize work, we also need to allocate time for our personal lives.

Many business apps focus on a particular medium, such as email or project boards. While these apps can be effective, they often lack integration with our personal schedules and don't consider the time we have available. For example, project management software may help us assign tasks, but it doesn't take into account how much time we have to coordinate to get our kids to activities and manage that other to-do list.

Many of these apps, such as a work Outlook calendar, focus on day-to-day tasks and reminders instead of the big picture. While it's important to stay on top of daily responsibilities, it's equally important to consider the holistic nature of our needs and how the different tasks involved in meeting these fit into our overall schedule.

By approaching our app usage with a Time Bandit mindset, we develop the ability to abstract our priorities from the systems of record. By all means make use of specific apps dedicated to a particular task type or function, but use your own system to arrange your priorities. Ultimately, productivity is best improved by having a broader view of priority management that guides your use of time and attention. The Time Bandit app is designed specifically to help you with this kind of priority management.

To achieve success in both short- and long-term battles, it's essential to break down your habits, tasks and projects into manageable chunks. This involves taking ownership of your responsibilities, determining when you need to complete different tasks and understanding the consequences if you cannot do so within the necessary timeframe. To do this, you need to break down your project work into individual tasks and account for them either individually or grouped as steps within a single task.

Tracking results

Keeping track of your progress can be straightforward, but if you have a particular interest in trends and data, you may prefer more detailed information. If you are using a commercially available platform, you'll likely have the option to access both simple reporting and more dynamic dashboard capabilities. Standard reporting typically functions as a completion or compliance tracker for the expected metrics. Keep in mind this isn't a data analysis project, but sometimes reflection is an excellent lesson for the future.

As mentioned earlier in the book, I use the Time Bandit habit tracker app to record my adherence to a particular habit with a simple tick each day. This creates a visual view of my progress toward establishing or breaking habits. Beyond this simple visual, you may be interested in a little more analysis of things like the percentage of your desired habits completed on a daily, weekly or monthly basis. It may also be able to motivate you by tracking your streaks.

See an example habit tracker below.

TRACKER

HABIT	S	M	T	W	T	F	S
1000 STEPS	V	V	V	V	V	V	V
PRACTICE SPANISH		V		V	V		V
READ 15 MIN	V	V		V	V	V	
TIME BANDIT	V	V	V	V	V	V	V
COLD CALLS		V		V		V	
NEAT HABIT	V	V				V	V

Task and project work

Routine tasks are typically viewable through the system of record that you use to schedule and track them. For instance, if you work in sales, your CRM system will be able to generate reports and dashboards that show the number of calls or emails sent to prospects in a specific period. Similarly, if you work in finance, you can likely access a report that shows the number of invoices processed. Ideally, most of these routine tasks will be part of a standard key performance indicator (KPI) or an objectives and key results (OKR) framework. One advantage of task management software or platforms, such as Asana or Smart Sheets, is that they often provide flexible dashboard capabilities. If these features are not available, you can always export your data to a spreadsheet and create your own dashboard in spreadsheets.

For the tasks that you are performing outside of BAU, you should look at a few metrics: tasks completed, tasks to be completed this day/week and certainly tasks that are potentially past due or contingent on others. You should be able to sort these tasks by role and by matrix category.

Most of the common task management platforms will allow you to filter and view your tasks in various ways, with 'list', 'board', or 'calendar' views being the most common. It should also be a requirement of your chosen task management app that it allows you to share tasks and assign them to others, attach documents or links and provide comments.

The **list view** is similar to a line on a spreadsheet, while the columns indicate various elements like due date, importance, urgency, role etc. Based on the Eisenhower Matrix categories, a board-style view provides a helpful visual representation of where to focus your time and energy with different cards on a larger board. For instance, you might create a card labeled 'Do Now' and list all tasks that fall into that category. Other cards might include 'Schedule', 'Delegate', and 'Stop/Park'. To better understand your level of success or the effort required for tasks ahead, it's also helpful to view the number of tasks completed, scheduled or even past due.

One useful feature of most task management apps is the ability for tasks to be easily moved from one card to another. This makes it easy to adjust priorities and keep your workload organized. By utilizing the card view, you'll get a clear view of what needs to be done and stay on track to achieve your goals.

The **calendar view** is probably the most common and straightforward way to manage tasks. It allows you to sort tasks by day, week or month and see those with specific due dates or scheduled for a particular time. This view is preferred by many who live and work by their schedule. However, some may find it overwhelming and not as effective.

There are a few other more specialized views that you may encounter. If available in your preferred app, a specific **Eisenhower Matrix view** offers a helpful overview of all presently active tasks, showing you the quadrants of the matrix and the number of items in each quadrant. A streaks feature appeals to me, as it highlights the need to prioritize a particular habit or type of task. Streaks, whether positive or negative, reflect the level of effort directed toward one's goals.

Whether you prefer a list, board or calendar view, the key is to use your chosen task/ time-management app in whatever way helps you stay organized and productive.

Time Bandit and supporting resources

We provide two key resources to support your efforts to be a Time Bandit: the Time Bandit app and Time Bandit Habit Tracker as well as other useful resources you will find using the QR code later in the book.

Time bandit app

I have a fascination with tech and finding the right solution to prioritize tasks and time, which is why we created the Time Bandit priority manager application that helps manage and guide your priorities efficiently. The app enables users to prioritize tasks into a corresponding list, providing a view of their tasks by role (work, personal, aspirational), by priority (Do Now, Schedule, Delegate, or Stop/Park) and associated with dates, attachments and other personalizations. This allows you to get into an easy daily rhythm, where you prioritize and act. Simplicity is oftentimes effective.

If you prefer not to use an app, we have also produced a simple alternative: a customized notepad. While it doesn't have built-in AI, for those who just want to organize by priority and continue working with their existing systems, it offers a low cost, low overhead way to get started with more efficient prioritizing.

Finally, for small businesses and workgroups that want to apply the Time Bandit method with their teams, we also provide coaching and implementation methods. We focus on practical applications with the tools you use for your team and the Time Bandit method.

The challenge with the commercial systems provided by your employer is that you do

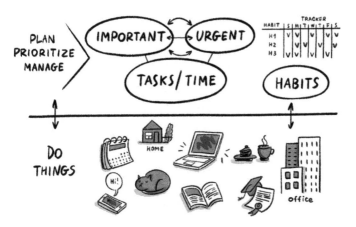

not want to put your personal or aspirational tasks in the system for all to see. This way, you can keep some tasks private, but be able to see your full set of tasks across all your roles (personal, work and aspirational). Many of the source systems and task management work a bit differently, but there is always a way to achieve the necessary integration to continue to prioritize your life in a manner that works with all the systems you're using and your Time Bandit preferences.

You may find shifting to an app to manage your time and tasks is an evolutional change. Personally, I used a pen and pad, then a spreadsheet, then moved to Microsoft Planner within Teams. Now, of course, I love the Time Bandit app, which interacts with my work Office 365 and other systems.

Time Bandit Habit Tracker

Additionally, we offer a free browser plug-in to provide an easy-to-use Habit Tracker. This asset is free to anyone. You will find it in your browser store or visit our website below for more details.

The Habit Tracker is a local browser plug-in that allows you to set up Habits to track for seven days (a weekly cadence). At the start of the next week, you can keep the streak going or add/delete habits at any time. While the tool is simple, the outcome can be significant. Small changes compound into big results over time. Tracking your habits is an easy way to hold yourself accountable.

Scan the QR code below to be directed to a Coterie Solutions/Time Bandit landing page. There you will find directions on how to get started based on your preferred approach. The team at Coterie can help you along the way, whether you need personalized coaching or simply want to use the digital training programs available.

Summary

We all need to balance our different responsibilities, whether they relate to work, family or personal aspirations. It's not always easy, but with careful planning and setting clear

priorities, we can achieve all our goals and find a sense of fulfillment in our lives. There's no need to be overwhelmed by the number of pro-ductivity tools available. Just focus on finding a balance that works for you – remember, you are in control of your own schedule.

SIX

The Power To Decide Your Future

Avoid wasting precious time on activities that may not align with your priorities. Instead, identify and address the time wasters that prevent you from achieving your goals and making the most of your time.

The importance of 'no'

One of the most crucial pieces of advice I can offer is to master the art of saying no. It's essential to decline things that aren't for you with a level head, compassion and balance, without being guided by anger or fear.

It's perfectly natural to feel anxious about certain tasks. But if the request is reasonable, relevant and your hesitation is because you're questioning your abilities, you should say yes and ask for more time or a mentor if necessary. Taking on new challenges and learning from them is an excellent way to expand your horizons.

Never say no to something based on emotion alone. Instead, consider your personal and professional aspirations before deciding. Of course, you should not agree to something that jeopardizes your well-being or your job performance – trust your intuition and values to guide you. If a requester is insistent and you feel cornered, I suggest you share your task list (or the relevant parts of it) with them and consider which items can be re-prioritized to make room for their task. If it affects others, consult with them about the potential delay and any costs or impacts that might arise.

By prioritizing effectively, you might find that you have more time on your hands. This doesn't mean you have to say yes to more things – take control, say no when you need to and enjoy the freedom that comes with it.

The real-world view

I work in sales. This industry can be a wild ride, with a constant stream of tasks, deadlines and expectations, but it offers high rewards for those who can handle the pressure. It can also break people and push them into alternative career paths.

Over the past eight years, I have been incredibly fortunate to work with an exceptional set of products and customers who are tackling the mammoth task of managing their time and work on a massive scale. Many of our customers, such as banks and insurance companies, provide services we use every day. These services require an immense amount of human labor to process the tasks involved in services like loans, claims and trades. Scheduling these resources is a challenge, and optimizing their time to meet the expectations of thousands of customers is truly a science.

We have helped some of the largest companies in the world take on this daunting challenge and succeed with flying colors. Our secret is that we understand the importance of preserving the well-being of the people who make these companies run. Contrary to popular belief, the most successful managers I have encountered prioritize employee needs before work demands. These are the teams that shine, not just in the short term, but in the long term too. The idea that successful managers are cold, calculating people who only care about production is a myth. In the real world, the most talented managers are those who recognize the value of investing in their people and creating a culture of positivity and productivity.

Effective strategies

An effective strategy to gain control of your time and focus on your tasks is to minimize interruptions and distractions. You can do this by turning off notifications for non-essential apps or emails, setting aside dedicated work time and communicating clear boundaries with co-workers and/or family members.

One common mistake people make that can rob them of time is confusing what should be a habit with a task on your to-do list. Some things should be habitual, part of a daily or weekly routine, rather than crowding other tasks that may have a specific deadline.

Procrastination is another common time waster that can have a significant impact on your available time. To overcome procrastination, it is important to understand the underlying reasons for it. Often, procrastination results from fear of failure or a misaligned importance factor. By breaking tasks into smaller, more manageable steps and establishing clear rewards for completing them, you can overcome procrastination and make better use of your time.

There are many tools and technologies that can help individuals manage these time wasters. For example, time-tracking apps can show you where your time is being spent, allowing you to make adjustments to your schedule or habits accordingly. Project management tools can also be helpful in breaking down complex tasks into smaller parts.

Ultimately, the way to make the most of your time is to anticipate and actively manage it. By establishing priorities, minimizing distractions and interruptions, and using tools and technologies to manage time more effectively, you can maximize the time you have available and achieve greater success in both your personal and professional lives.

Balance

Since the Covid-19 pandemic, there has been an overwhelming amount of discussion surrounding work–life balance. Why has this become such a popular topic? Technology enabled us to merge our work and personal lives and create a new way of living, but now we must find a way to balance our family, work and personal lives while also incorporating things like exercise to escape the stresses of other parts of life and protect our health and well-being.

As you implement Time Bandit, you will discover two things. First, you will be amazed at how many things you need and want to do. Second, you will become an expert at prioritizing your tasks. It's essential to find balance in our lives, and time management is crucial in achieving this. With effective time blocking and prioritization, you can create a schedule that allows you to focus on your priorities and navigate between your personal and professional life.

The key to success with Time Bandit is to approach it with a pragmatic mindset. While motivation and willpower have their place, alone they are not sufficient nor sustainable in the long term. To achieve balance, you need to be realistic and practical. You may have to re-order tasks, pass on some duties, or just park certain projects. It's important to remember that what this balance looks like is up to you, and not to stress about it. When feeling overwhelmed, take a step back, re-prioritize and then focus on your new priorities. By clearing your schedule and getting a task done without interruption, you'll feel successful and motivated, which will help you get back into the rhythm you need to achieve your goals. By setting boundaries and practicing mindfulness, you can also reduce the impact of interruptions and distractions and stay focused on your work.

There are experts who can help you prioritize your health and goals if you need support with this. If you're struggling to find a balance in your personal and professional life and this is having a negative impact on your health and well-being, seek their guidance.

Summary

We have explored a variety of strategies for managing time wasters, including categorizing and prioritizing tasks, using habit tracking, avoid distraction and procrastination, and establishing a steady rhythm.

By understanding urgency and importance, we can better understand how we need to prioritize our time. When we have a clear sense of our priorities, we are less likely to get sidetracked by activities that do not align with our goals. Using time blocks can help us stay focused and productive, while delegating responsibilities can free up our time to focus on more important tasks. Managing interruptions and avoiding distractions is also key. Ultimately, managing your time requires a combination of self-awareness, discipline and honesty. It may not be easy, but the rewards of effective priority management make it more than worthwhile.

Time is a finite resource that you cannot afford to waste. By identifying and addressing the wasters in your life and habits, you can prioritize your time and achieve your goals. Let the matrix guide your time usage and turn your priorities into allies and achieve your full potential. Now get out there and be your own

Time Bandit – take back control and 'Do Now' the things that matter most.

Time Bandit is available for iPhone, iPad or MacOS. It is also available for Android devices, and you can find it on the Google Play store.

Author

 Michael Cupps (known as Cupps) has been in technology sales for over thirty years, starting with a dial-up modem and making his way through eight acquisitions and mergers, experiencing the volatile tech industry across many sectors, from information security to content management, business process management and social and workforce

productivity software. For most of his career he has led teams in sales and marketing, but he has also developed and managed large business development programs with various partners.

Regardless of individual or team efforts, Cupps' focus has always been on overachieving. He has recently made his voice heard through social channels and news articles on topics such as the four-day work week, productivity management and remote working. He has also appeared on many radio and television interviews to speak about similar topics, and is the host of AO on Air podcast.

Cupps was born and raised as a native Texan and grew up on a small farm/ranch that was self-sufficient in raising crops and cattle. These early years taught him the value of hard work, priorities and managing time wisely. He obtained his Bachelor of Science in International Trade from Texas Tech University.

Cupps still enjoys spending time with family on the lakes in Texas or on any beach, walking his dog, Oliver, and spending time with his love, Catherine. His current aspiration is to learn French, Catherine's native language, which he practices on frequent trips to Catherine's home and other French-speaking islands. A colon cancer survivor, Cupps is happy to share and offer his guidance to others who have experienced this disease, advocating for early screening.

Cupps considers himself lucky to have worked in unique and productive spaces and is proud to share his knowledge and experience. Most of all, he wants to help you be a productive Time Bandit, reduce your anxiety and generate more time for the good stuff.

- 🌐 www.coteriesolutions.com
- ⓕ www.facebook.com/coteriesolutions
- ⓘ www.linkedin.com/company/coterie -solutions/
- ⓧ @coterieSolutio1